I0755945

FINISHING LINE PRESS
www.finishinglinepress.com

Can you see her, the moon?

poems by

Erika Nichols-Frazer

Finishing Line Press
Georgetown, Kentucky

Can you see her, the moon?

ISBN 979-8-89990-508-7 First Edition

ACKNOWLEDGMENTS

"A Holy Thing" was originally published in the *PoemCity 2025* anthology
"Summer of Smoke" was originally published in the *PoemCity 2024* anthology
"an exercise in trying not to cry" was originally published in *The Mountain Troubadour*
"Easy" and "Solar Eclipse" were originally published in a locally distributed anthology, *PoemTown Randolph*

Publisher: Leah Huete de Maines
Editor: Christen Kincaid
Cover Art: Dylan Frazer
Author Photo: Erika Nichols-Frazer
Cover Design: Elizabeth Maines McCleavy

Order online: www.finishinglinepress.com
also available on amazon.com

Author inquiries and mail orders:
Finishing Line Press
PO Box 1626
Georgetown, Kentucky 40324
USA

Contents

For Dylan, who has been with me every step of the way.
I like you & I love you.

And for Arden, whose adventures are just beginning.

Author's Note

I want to acknowledge that the content of this collection may be difficult for some, particularly those who have experienced trauma, including pregnancy loss, or who have struggled with reproductive health, choice, childbirth, or anything pertaining to the decision of what your family looks like. You are not alone and do not need to suffer in silence. I hope that these words can be a support to you but please be kind to yourself; step away when you need to. Know that our journeys are not always simple and linear. Know that you are not alone. Know that you are stronger than you may think. Take care.

A Holy Thing

A mouth is a holy thing,
Fistful of thickets,
Sponge-tongued,
Cavernous—

Consumes.

A body is a holy thing—
What it chooses,
What is done to it,
What it

Becomes.

Naked strength, power.

Not holy as in Biblical or rite.

As in fever.
As in want.
As in fire.

Expecting

April 2

I want   this   more
than   I've ever   wanted

          anything.

Streaks
          a good thing
          once.
Now   possible sign
          of   [ ]

The crying comes again.

The doctor reassured me, but   I don't feel

                                        safe.

Rest,   she said
                                        take it easy.

As if   this   is   easy.

                    Want

The hardest thing.

April 3

The dreary day reflects my   (fear)
anxiety hungry.

I would pray if I believed in   a god.

Instead, I beg—

Let this be real.

Let it be mine.

April 6

Red

I count the red things in the room like the book on trauma said—

The stand-up mixer my husband gave me for Christmas
the first year of the pandemic when I was baking a lot.
The trim on the placemats with chickens strutting
across them (when you own chickens, everyone gifts you
things with chickens on them), the caps on spice jars,
the plastic mechanical arm a friend gave us as a joke,
several book covers, a magnet on the fridge.

The fact that the blood is not red is a good sign,
the doctor paged on a Sunday said.
I tried to believe her.

Red in the abstract "portrait" of me on the wall,
painted by a friend, titled "Warrior Woman,"
my husband's nickname for me. I don't feel much
of a Warrior now. Vulnerable. Weak.

Red on the label of the bread bag that contains
his homemade sourdough. Red on the dish towel,
the cap of vodka no one drinks.

Please, not red, I beg no one. *Please.*

April 8

By myself in the ER—

It got worse.

Couldn't take it anymore, paged
the on-call doctor first thing
on a Saturday, balls of soggy tissues
on my nightstand, coffee table, floor.
Brought the box of tissues with me
as I drove the hour to the ER, balled
up tear-soaked tissues tossed in the backseat.

My husband away, so I am
alone.
Nearly five hours in the hospital, a parade
of nurses, questions.
Blood pressure, weight,
heartrate, IV, ultrasound, shot of Rhogam.
Wheelchairs me through a maze.

I can't hear the heartbeat, the technician says, and
everything stops—my heart—
but then she says, *But I can see it, the heartbeat,*
It's there.

We listen to blood
flow in my ovaries, waves crashing on shore.

Alive, someone says. *Alive.*

April 12

You wouldn't be human if you weren't worried,
The doctor told me, the ancient one,

which didn't make me any less worried
but did make me feel more human.

Good signs, he said. *These are good signs.*

April 17

Grey, the absence of color,
Sky empty,
Spring rain, our porch littered
with chicken shit, trees beyond the yard
nearly ready to bloom, my heart bursting,
my womb—
Somber, grey, lonely.
awaiting the colors,
yellow blurs and bursts of orange,
smears of red, pops of pink
against the greyness,   a spark.

April 20

From the clouds, a shaft of sunlight,
The weight of a gentle dog's head in
a soft lap, closed eyes, heartbeat.

The quiet in a storm.

April 27

They gave me a lollipop, the kind kids get
at the doctor's office. The kind we used to buy
with our pennies at the general store.
Grape, my least favorite flavor. A meager condolence.

Now, when I fill out forms at the doctor's office,
under 'number of pregnancies,' I'll have to write 'two'
and under 'number of children,' 'zero.' That thought
depresses me almost as much as the thought
of calling the childcare center to take us off the
waiting list (though my husband volunteered to do
that) or deleting the pregnancy app from my phone.

Someone at the OB office called to ask why I cancelled
my next appointment, which I had done via the app while I waited
in the blood lab's waiting room, where they asked how I was doing
today.
An impossible answer. Bawling. No tissues. People staring.
The call came as I drove myself home from the hospital, sobbing.
When the words came out, the person on the other end of the line
said,
"Disregard this phone call."

April 28

The dress taunts me from the closet.
The shimmery gold-green gown
I bought in XL because I thought I'd be
eight months pregnant by the time of our friends' wedding.
Optimistic thinking.

And now, I'm not pregnant anymore and that
gorgeous dress, just staring at me,
will sit there in the closet, forgotten,
like the future we thought we held in our hands.

April 30

A thing I learned:
When you have a miscarriage, people give you plants.
Something else to nurture into growing, I guess.
A peace lily, pink potted flowers, a bouquet of pink
roses and lilies. Growth everywhere, as I wait for
the blood to pass. The doctor says it like that,
to pass, as if it's a simple, non-violent thing.

Another thing I learned:
Strangers feel comfortable asking you
to relive your trauma, thinking you
will be excited to share your good news.

When they told me there was no more heartbeat—
Gone silent—
I felt it was inevitable, that this was what I had
feared was coming, that my anxiety and panic
attacks had been right. This did not assuage the pain.

No one was there with me. The most alone I'd ever felt.

How long is it acceptable to mourn? How can I move on?

Un-

After Leila Chatti

wanted
viable
done

stable
filtered

available

empathetic

finished

imaginable

trying not to think about it,

it's all i can think about.
don't cry, don't surrender to your emotions;
this rarely works.

reminders are everywhere though i am
trying not to think about it,
the memories my body holds, that take over.
don't cry.

the memories my body holds take over.
i had once wished for blood then cursed it,
then prayed for it (as if I believed in prayer)
                    to pass, to be over.
don't cry.

                    "you're alone in there now,"
                    the technician tells me, and I guess
                    that's what we were hoping for,
                    at this point.

i had once wished for blood then cursed it,
prayed, the piece of myself disappearing, no control.
you're alone in there now
what we were hoping for, at this point.

the piece of myself disappearing, echoing:
alone in there, emotional pain manifested in my body

blood proof of what I have lost,
what I cannot get back.

The Summer of Smoke

Wildfires consume the north, closing in.
Haze obscures the mountain view from our home,
a former weekend ski cabin for flatlanders. Now ours.

Haze obscures my thoughts, too, shifting and impossible to grasp,
like smoke. It's been more than two months and the pain has not
abated, perhaps dulled a bit, like an old kitchen knife, still full of hurt.

I mourn something that never was, a life I did not have, a life that will
never be.
It's impossible to see clearly, impossible to imagine it will ever change.
The haze will be here all summer, they say. Perhaps longer for me.

Water does not bring relief, nor do the things people say. Normal.
Common.
At least.

Fires rage, inside and out. Tears come easily now.

How do we clear the fog, see through the smoke? How will I heal?

How long will this go on?

Easy

It worries me now, how easy
it is to die. A swerve
to the left or a step off
the curb, only a lonely ripple
to announce that I had once existed,
been *right there*, under the dark waters
that swallowed me.
This happens as you get older, people say,
but I was young when I began imagining
my early, violent death. Not once, but all the time.
I thought I deserved it.
As the leaves decay in backyard piles—worm-full,
probably ticks, too—I see death before me,
marching closer each day, rolling out
the red carpet for winter, for the snows to come
and wipe us all clean. I die a little each day.
So do we all.
People say things:
Fleeting, precious, et cetera.
To hold it in your hand, to claim it as your own:

A miracle.

Solar Eclipse

Can you see her, the moon,
her embrace of the sun,
her distant love, burning white hot
in the craters of her cold, rocky heart?
I know she's there, even if not visible
under my sky.

Squint, view indirectly, from a distance.
Don't let the colliding burn you up
(as if you control anything).

I am small under this miracle.
We might miss it, but it's there,
which is not a small comfort.

Despair

Tell me about despair, yours, and I will tell you mine.
Meanwhile the world goes on.
—Mary Oliver, "Wild Geese"

Some days, the weight is too heavy to carry.
But how can I complain? Is it selfish to worry
over my problems, which belong only to me,
while children die in Gaza, in Sudan, Ethiopia, Ukraine?
While children starve, fear, sleep in streets?

I suffer, you suffer, they suffer, we suffer.
Do the varying shades of our suffering separate
or unite us?

Women carry pain, carry babies, lose homes, lose marriages, lose babies
(as if they have been misplaced). Women suffer. Women fear for their lives,
are raped, beaten, tortured. Black children murdered. Trans kids bullied, attacked,
pushed too far. I justify, at least it's not that, *at least.*

Can my pain, which seems so small compared to the world, also be real
while so many people suffer, hurt, die?
What is the weight of my loss? How long am I allowed to mourn
the life I held in my hands, that had rooted in my body?
Will it diminish the joy of my loved ones? Will it insult someone
else whose pain is larger, heavier? Can I hold pain and empathy in both hands?

Let us not compare, but stand, holding our hearts out
in silence when the words won't come, in solidarity.

an exercise in trying not to cry

Bite your lip.
Deep breaths.
Drink a glass of ice water slowly.

Turn on Bright Eyes or Noah Kahan
or something else that makes you
sad.

Cry anyway.
Lie on the couch, pull a blanket over
Yourself, the one your great-grandmother
knit.

Close your eyes.

Cuddle with the dogs, scritch their bellies,
let them lick your face, your tears.
Call your best friend then feel bad
because she's trying to put the baby down
for a nap. Think of people you can call then
cry more at how short the list is, the reasons
you won't call.

Consider posting on social media
asking for hugs, hope, good vibes, but don't.
Too many questions. You don't need pity,
Just someone to listen.

Cry for a while. Then get the fuck up.

Dear Ruth Bader Ginsberg, or Dead Chickens

The worst winter in years, they're calling it,
just months after the second "500-year flood"
in a decade.

Climate change, says one of the spandex-ed cyclists
stopped on the side of my road in a cluster. The others nod.
They don't move while my car bounces down the rutted dirt road.
I swerve away from them and almost get stuck twice.

The fourth or fifth mud season this year,
men in flannel sipping fresh coffee in our local
grocery say. Unusual, we all agree, but it is clear that

things are getting worse across the board.

Something got into the chicken coop last night, a weasel, most
likely, or a small fisher, dragged the slightly-off-kilter board
weighed down by a brick and a heavy piece of cement out of the way.
Feasted.
I must have left a small gap when I closed the chickens up
for the night in the dark. I'd forgotten my headlamp, I realized
half-way to the coop as I stumbled over the uneven mound
of dirt gathered in the well-trodden path. The drainage in the yard needs
fixing, my husband explains, the swamp consuming the area behind the
coop.
My glittered muck boots suck in every time, make an unsettling squelch
when I try to lift my leg. I feel blindly in the dark.

All the chickens died, one of whom we'd had for eight years,
and it was my fault. The fetus died and what if that was my fault, too?
What if I can't nurture anything right?
What if I carry death with me?

What can be done?

Her name was Ruth, the oldest chicken,
or maybe Bader, because we couldn't actually

distinguish between chickens, just knew we started
off with three Buff Orpingtons—plump, butter
yellows—and three Golden-Laced Wyandottes—
glossy feathers shimmering brown-gold
in the afternoon light, as they pecked at worms and sod.
Then came the Barred Rocks, the Americaunas.

We named the first batch in threes—Ruth, Bader, and Ginsburg
for the Orpingtons, and Julia, Louis, and Dreyfus for the Wyandottes.
Their names were interchangeable. Symbol of strength. Taking no
shit.
Then, after some gruesome losses, we stopped naming the new ones.
More came.
Now, they are all gone.

Dear Ruth, I am sorry I could not protect you
how your namesake fought to protect so many.

What lurks by the coop, waiting for some careless woman
stumbling through the dark, the small opening she will leave that will
invite death in?

I could not look at their bodies. I asked my husband
if he needed help discarding them, hoping he'd say no, which he did.
Then I watched from the living room, through the new glass doors
that are still broken, see the thick curtain of smoke
from their bodies mingle in a funeral pyre with the corpse of our
dried Christmas tree, the one we left up until January 31 this year.
I just couldn't bring myself to part with it,
its glimmering lights and the magic of innocence.

I have always had a hard time parting.

This is the hard part about having animals.
My dogs are ailing, old. We will say goodbye to one soon.
A heavy decision, to let her go.
The other had surgery to remove the cancerous tumor yesterday

and now she is bumping into things with her translucent
cone—the kitchen island, a chair, the coffee table.
She has no sense of the space she takes up, no
awareness beyond herself, beyond the pain.

I understand, Dear One. I, too, have been vanquished
by pain. How can I decide when to start or end a life?
Who gave me the right, the responsibility?

We will build a new coop from what we can salvage of
rotting wood in a muddy pit. We will order more chicks
from the farm store this spring. We take the week off from
work to keep an eye on the cancerous dog, to help
ease her pain. As if there is anything we can do
but tell her to *ride it out, baby; take it easy; sleep,*
wait for the pain to ease.

We give her a treat, scritch her scruffy neck, lay our
heads heavy on her belly while she breathes—in, out.
To witness. Try again.

With Thanks

So many people were an integral part of my healing journey and the process of creating this book.

First and foremost, my husband, Dylan, who has supported me through everything and pushed me (in the kindest, gentlest of ways) to write my way through it, who kept the house going while I struggled to get out of bed. Thank you, my love. I am eternally grateful for your partnership and everything you do. Also, thanks for being my official photographer.

Kelsey G. Dunn also deserves all my gratitude and thanks. I don't know how I'd get through this life without your lifelong friendship. Thanks to everyone who has checked in with me over the years and been there, even if they didn't realize how much it meant to me.

To all my family and friends who have supported me along the way, supported my writing, and encouraged me; my deepest thanks.

To the organizers of *PoemCity* Montpelier and *PoemTown* Randolph, especially Sam Kolber, publisher of *PoemCity*'s anthologies, as well as the Poetry Society of Vermont, where some of these poems first appeared; thank you for giving me a space to be heard.

To everyone at the Bennington Writing Seminars; thank you for teaching me so much about writing and about myself. To my dear Renegade Writers over the years (Shelagh, Niels, Patrick, LeeAnn, Mark, Angi, Kate, Jess, Kim), the best writers' group a girl could ask for; thank you for your friendship and insights. They have been invaluable.

Thank you to Kellam Ayres, Sarah Audsley, and Elaine Pentaleri for your kind words.

Thanks as well to the entire Vermont literary community, which I've had the pleasure of being a part of—the organizers of Green Mountain Book Fest and Bookstock, Vermont Studio Center, librarians, independent booksellers, and everyone who works to keep the literary arts in our region alive and vibrant.

And thank you to Arden for making me a mama, for teaching me a new kind of love.

Erika Nichols-Frazer (she/her) is the author of the memoir, *Feed Me: A Story of Food, Love and Mental Illness* (Casper Press, 2022), the poetry collection, *Staring Too Closely* (Main Street Rag, 2023), and the short story collection *No One Will Ever Hear You* (Rootstock Publishing, 2026). She holds an MFA from the Bennington Writing Seminars and a BA in Liberal Arts from Sarah Lawrence College. Her poems, essays, and short stories have been published in various journals, including *HuffPost, River Teeth's "Beautiful Things," Gone Lawn, Emerge Literary Journal, Bloodroot Literary Magazine, Idle Ink, Bright Flash Literary Review, Lunate, Burningword Literary Journal*, and others. She won Noir Nation's 2020 Golden Fedora Fiction Prize and has been nominated for a Pushcart Prize.

Erika has worked as an editor, journalist, nonprofit development director, and taught writing to students of all ages in a variety of settings, including at the Governor's Institutes of Vermont, Central Vermont Adult Education, libraries, book festivals, and elsewhere. She owns Good Wolf Literary Services and works at Vermont State University. She lives in Vermont with her husband, daughter, and various animals. She can be found at *nicholsfrazer.com*.

www.ingramcontent.com/pod-product-compliance
Lightning Source LLC
LaVergne TN
LVHW090542110826
845146LV00003B/1234
* 9 7 9 8 8 9 9 9 0 5 0 8 7 *